The VANISHING MANATEE

Manatees at play Patrick M. Rose

The VANISHING MANATEE

Margaret Goff Clark

Illustrated with photographs

Cobblehill Books
Dutton / New York

For Jeffrey Charles Clark
I hope there'll be manatees in your future

PHOTOGRAPH CREDITS: Garth Francis/*News Press*, 58; Courtesy
Miami Seaquarium, 55; Thomas J. O'Shea, 19; Courtesy Sea World
of Florida, 40. All other photographs are by Patrick M. Rose.

Library of Congress Cataloging-in-Publication Data
Clark, Margaret Goff.
   The vanishing manatee / Margaret Goff Clark.
      p.   cm.
   Summary: Introduces the playful manatee and discusses its
future and its relationship with humans.
   ISBN 0-525-65024-5
   1. Manatees—Juvenile literature. [1. Manatees. 2. Rare
animals. 3. Wildife conservation.] I. Title.
QL737.S63C53   1990
599.5'5—dc20   89-38676   CIP   AC

Published in the United States by Cobblehill Books,
an affiliate of Dutton Children's Books, a division
of Penguin Books USA Inc.
Published simultaneously in Canada by
Fitzhenry & Whiteside Limited, Toronto
Designed by Mina Greenstein
Printed in Hong Kong
First Edition   10 9 8 7 6 5 4 3 2 1

Acknowledgments

The author wishes to thank the following for their help:

Patrick M. Rose, Marine Mammals Coordinator, Florida Marine Research Institute, Department of Natural Resources (DNR), for reading the manuscript and writing the Introduction.

Also from the DNR: R. Kipp Frohlich, Marine Mammal Biologist; Jan Wright, Manatee Information Specialist.

Dr. Thomas J. O'Shea, Sirenia Project Leader of the National Ecology Research Center under the U.S. Fish & Wildlife Service, who checked the manuscript.

The people at Sea World of Florida, who helped in many ways, especially Dr. Daniel K. Odell, Research Biologist, who checked the final manuscript; Ed Asper, Vice President and Zoological Director of Sea World Enterprises, and Frank Murru, Vice President and General Curator for Sea World of Florida, who were particularly helpful in the early stages; and Nick Gollattscheck, Public Relations, Senior Representative, who tirelessly answered questions and supplied information.

Dr. Jesse White, formerly Veterinarian at the Miami Seaquarium, and wife, Diane, both of whom told me about their work in captive breeding.

J. P. Garner, Park Manager, Homosassa Springs State Park.

Judith D. Vallee, Administrator, Save the Manatee Club.

Major Denis Grealish of the Florida Marine Patrol.

Dr. Gary Nelson, DVM, Fort Myers, Florida, Veterinarian.

The Nature Center and Planetarium of Lee County, Florida.

South Florida Museum and Planetarium at Bradenton, Florida, home of forty-one-year-old Snooty, oldest living manatee born in captivity.

Noel and Bert MacCarry for their informal manatee news clipping service.

Contents

Introduction

Margaret Goff Clark's *The Vanishing Manatee* introduces the reader to one of Florida's and, indeed, the United States' most lovable and endearing creatures, the manatee. It was a true pleasure to read her book and think about how it would awaken young and old alike to the wonders and perils of the endangered manatee's world. The manatee is the barometer of Florida's future. Preserving the manatee and its habitat is to preserve Florida for future generations.

PATRICK M. ROSE
Marine Mammals Coordinator
Florida Marine Research Institute
Department of Natural Resources

Close-up of a manatee coming to the surface for air   Patrick M. Rose

Encounter
with a Giant

I sat in a canoe on the Orange River in southwestern Florida in December and watched manatee noses appear and disappear all around me. Each one looked like a cow's nose with breathing holes on top of the wide snout.

Nearby, an enormous dark gray back rose out of the water and then humped down in a dive that ended with a flourish of a tail like a giant Ping-Pong paddle. I held my breath while the huge, silent animal swam beneath my canoe. The average manatee is about ten feet long and weighs about 1,000 pounds. Adults may reach a weight of 3,000 pounds. Biologists weighed one at 3,650 pounds. The one swimming near me was as long as my canoe and possessed a powerful tail. It could easily tip over my craft and send me flying.

I was relieved when its blimp-shaped form disappeared in the distance, although I knew this friendly giant would not hurt me on purpose. The manatee has never been known to attack, even to save its own life. Since it had few, if any, natural enemies, it did not develop a habit of defending itself. Some people have claimed that such creatures as sharks and crocodiles are its enemies, but manatee expert, Dr. Daniel S. Hartman, wrote that this had not been proved.

More recently, however, Dr. Thomas J. O'Shea, Sirenia Project Leader of the National Ecology Research Center under the U.S. Fish & Wildlife Service, reported hearing from a reliable source while doing research in Panama that shark attacks did occur. Dr. O'Shea said, "We also saw a shark bite on one from the Crystal River. No other instances of predation on manatees are known."

Besides being friendly, the manatee also is curious. People who fish in the Caloosahatchee River in southwestern Florida have reported visits from manatees that lingered and, with their small, round eyes, seemed to study the boat and the people in it.

One manatee even clung to the anchor line, using its front flippers like short arms while it checked out the rope with its mouth. Not many are that tame, but most are quite trusting, sometimes more trusting than is healthy for them.

During a visit to the Miami Seaquarium I became better acquainted with these little-known creatures.

Crouching on a platform just above the surface of the pool

Two manatee faces at close range Patrick M. Rose

where three manatees were swimming, I held out one of the pieces of food given to me by Dr. Jesse White, then the staff veterinarian.

The food looked like a bone-shaped dog biscuit. Dr. Dan Odell, Research Biologist at Sea World, has since explained to me that these were zoo monkey biscuits.

At once a manatee was in front of me, and when it took the biscuit, its mouth closed around my hand. I was surprised at the soft smoothness inside its lips as compared with the stiff bristles outside. It made no effort to bite my hand or spit it out.

I later found out that manatees have six to seven molar teeth in each of four rows, two upper, two lower, that arise in the back of the jaw. These gradually move forward, and as they are worn down by chewing on the often sandy vegetation, they fall out and are replaced by new teeth.

While I continued to feed the manatee, I noticed its bristly upper lip was split and that it moved strongly to seize the food and maneuver it into its mouth. At one point the animal poked a morsel in place with a flipper.

Even after my supply of biscuits was gone, this friendly creature stayed beside me while I stroked its leathery, rather rough head. At first I thought it had no ears. Then I saw the small ear opening about ten inches behind each eye.

No one could overlook the stiff whiskers on its face and around its mouth, but on its head and body there were only scattered hairs.

Feeding or touching a manatee in the wild is not a good idea, I learned, and there is a law forbidding it. If the animal finds it can look to man for food and petting, it may be even less likely to flee from motorboats and from vandals who might harm it on purpose.

Manatees are not in danger from the wild animals they encounter, but in many ways man is their deadly enemy.

Just what is a manatee and from where did it come?

A Family History

In 1493, when Christopher Columbus was visiting the New World, he reported seeing three mermaids, and wrote in his journal, "They are not so beautiful as they are painted."

It is believed what he saw must have been manatees, for they frequent the waters around the island of Haiti, the area where Columbus was when he wrote this entry. Viewed from the deck of a ship, a mother manatee with her calf nursing behind her flipper might have faintly resembled a mermaid.

The manatee is a gray or grayish-brown aquatic mammal most often found in water from three to ten feet deep.

Powered by a flat tail, it cruises underwater with nostrils

Powered by its tail, the manatee swims to the surface.   Patrick M. Rose

closed, coming up approximately every three to five minutes to breathe. As soon as its nose rises above the surface, the nostrils open. The manatee breathes out and in, the nostrils close, and it dives headfirst, sometimes breaking water with its back and tail.

It is often called a sea cow because it grazes on underwater pastures.

There are three species of manatee today, the West Indian, the West African, and the Amazonian. All belong to an order of mammals called Sirenia, which also includes the dugong and the now extinct Steller's sea cow. The name Sirenia comes from the word "siren." A Greek myth claimed a siren was a female creature who lured sailors to their death by her beautiful singing.

Probably the dugong was the basis for the siren legend. Early navigators to India and China saw them, for they were once plentiful in warm waters along the shores of the Indian Ocean and western Pacific.

Dugongs cannot sing but, like the manatee, they nurse their young. Did a sailor at the helm of a boat, sighting a dugong mother with her offspring suckling behind a flipper, stare too long and crash his boat onto the rocks?

It is thought the closest living relatives of the Sirenia are the elephant and the hyrax, a rabbit-sized rodentlike plant-eating animal that lives in Africa. Scientists believe all of these mammals share the same ancestor that lived on Earth millions of years ago. It had four legs and ate grasses and plants. The elephant developed from this creature and stayed on land. So did the hyrax.

Unlike the elephant and hyrax, the Sirenia gradually adapted to the water. Their front legs became flippers, the hind legs disappeared, and a new structure, the tail paddle, developed.

In the case of the West Indian and West African manatee, there is a forelimb inside each flipper, as well as three or more toenails on the outside. There are no visible divisions for toes.

Sirenians are the only marine mammals, except for whales and dolphins, that spend their entire lives in the water, and the only marine mammals that feed exclusively on vegetation.

The West Indian manatee (*Trichechus manatus*) lives in Florida, the coastal waters and rivers of islands in the Caribbean Sea, and along the Atlantic coast of South America as far south as northeastern Brazil. Fossil records show the manatee has been in Florida for millions of years. Apparently it flourished, unmolested, until the coming of man. All it needed was water no colder than 68 degrees F and plenty of underwater grasses to eat. It can live in both salt water and fresh, traveling from lakes and rivers to shallow coastal water.

This manatee is feeding on a plant at the bottom of a stream.   Patrick M. Rose

A West African manatee. Note the bristles and wide nostrils.

When people arrived, they killed the manatee for its tasty flesh, its bone, its high quality oil, and the hide which made good leather. Although in the United States the manatee is now rarely hunted for food or for other uses, its existence is still in jeopardy.

The West African manatee (*Trichechus senegalensis*) lives along the coast and in the rivers of western Africa. It is very similar to the West Indian manatee in appearance and habits. It, too, lives in both salt water and fresh, and is hunted for food, its oil, and hide. Like all Sirenians, the West African manatee is in danger of vanishing from the earth.

The Amazonian manatee (*Trichechus inunguis*) differs most

from the other two. It has no toenails and is the only one that lives all the time in fresh water. Also, since bottom grasses do not grow well in the rivers where it stays, it has adapted to eating the plentiful floating plants.

From early days until the present, the flesh of the Amazonian manatee has been a regular part of the diet of the natives of northern South America. *Mixira*, manatee meat, cooked in its own blubber, stays fresh for months.

When the first European colonists, the missionaries, arrived in Brazil, they provided another market for manatee meat. Believing the creature to be a fish because it lived in the water, they recommended its flesh be eaten on Friday, the day when faithful Catholics did not eat meat.

In the seventeenth century, shiploads of manatee meat crossed to Europe. Even in this century, in one twenty-year period, approximately 200,000 Amazonian manatees were killed, mainly for their skins which were used for leather.

Since the middle 1970s, a study has been going on in Manaus, Brazil. Orphaned manatee calves are captured and raised in captivity. Caring for and observing these calves, scientists are learning more about their growth and behavior than it was possible to discover in the wild, where they swim beneath a thick blanket of water plants.

Other studies are being made of the usefulness of this manatee in clearing floating weeds from tropical man-made lakes.

The other living member of the order Sirenia, the dugong (*Dugong dugon*), also makes water its home.

The dugong is strictly a marine animal, often spending the day in deep water and swimming close to shore in early evening to feed. It can reach a length of thirteen feet, including a tail forked like a whale's. It weighs from 500 to 2,000 pounds. The upper lip is not divided like that of the manatee, but it has a useful horseshoe-shaped disc at the end of its snout which helps in digging up the roots of the underwater plants it likes. It also has two upper incisors which in the male develop into stubby tusks.

Because it lives mainly in the open seas, instead of in rivers as the manatee does, the dugong is less subject to accidental death or injury by propellers or collision with ships and barges. Yet it is shadowed by a greater danger. For centuries it has been hunted for its meat, hide, and short tusks. This is continuing today.

The fifth Sirenian, Steller's sea cow, was the only one of the group to adapt to cold water. In the icy Bering Sea some grew to more than thirty feet long with a waistline of twenty feet and a weight of about seven tons.

Living in herds, they slept just offshore, with their young in the center of a circle of mature males and females. When the tide swept in, they came in with it to eat the marine algae from the rocks near the beach. It is thought that what they ate was the giant kelp.

These peaceful giants were discovered in 1741 by Russian explorers led by a Danish navigator, Vitus Bering. The mission of the explorers was to find the location of America in relation to Asia. After glimpsing Alaska, they were on their way home when their ship, the *St. Peter*, was caught in storms and went ashore on what is now called Bering Island.

It was winter and the *St. Peter* was breaking up. The cold, hungry men soon discovered it was easy to wade into the shallow water and kill the placid sea cows. Eating the creatures' flesh helped to save the men's lives.

One person on this expedition was Georg Wilhelm Steller, a German who was educated in botany and medicine. He was interested in the sea cow beyond its usefulness as food. Because of its appearance and habits, he knew it must be a relative of the tropical manatee.

Steller's careful notes give us a picture of this biggest member of the Sirenia order. He said its flippers were clublike, with stiff bristles on the soles. Its skin, Steller said, was thick, like "the bark of an ancient oak."

This observant man also noted that sea cows tried to help each other when there was danger and would stay for days beside the body of a mate that had died.

When warm weather returned, the men built a small vessel from the remains of the *St. Peter*, and sailed back to Siberia. Their tales of the fur seals, sea otters, and blue foxes they had seen on their voyage sent fur hunters to the Aleutian Islands off the coast of Alaska. On the way, these hunters stopped on Bering Island and nearby Copper Island to stock up on meat.

Constant hunting brought about the end of Steller's sea cow. It has not been seen since 1768.

Although Georg Wilhelm Steller sent his report on the big marine mammal to the Russian ruler, he received no praise for his valuable observations. Steller was no longer alive when the creature he had studied was given his name.

More than two hundred years passed before a trained, caring person like Steller arrived to study and describe the manatee.

The World
of the Manatee

It has taken people a long time to learn about the manatee.

For thousands of years native tribes in Florida and the Caribbean area hunted manatees. So did explorers and settlers from Europe who followed Columbus, but except for its meat and hide, no one seemed interested in the animal itself.

As time went on, scientists dissected dead manatees to study the skeleton and internal organs, but the living creature remained a mystery.

In the 1950s a biologist named J.D. Moore did some manatee studies, observing them from the surface of the water.

It was another biologist, Daniel S. Hartman, a graduate student at Cornell University, who dived into the water with the manatees and became acquainted with them. In 1967 he made them the subject of study for his doctoral degree.

After a survey of the Florida coasts, he chose King's Bay in the Crystal River in the western part of the state for his labo-

The rebreather apparatus worn by this biologist/diver limits the bubbles that come from scuba gear and frighten manatees. Patrick M. Rose

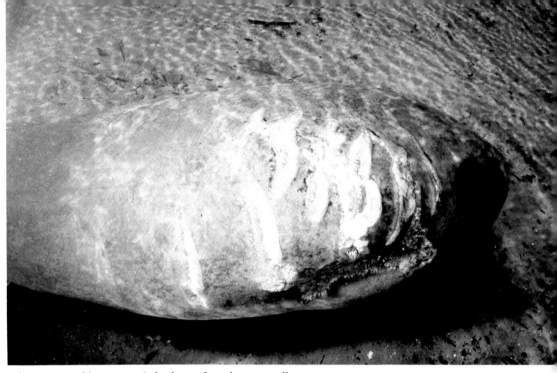

The scars on this manatee's back are from boat propellers. Patrick M. Rose

ratory. A skin diver's wet suit, face mask, and flippers made up his uniform.

Day after day Hartman swam with the manatees or floated above them in a small boat, watching the way they looked, what they ate, and how they spent their time. Some ignored this friendly stranger, while others accepted him so wholeheartedly they hugged him with their flippers and planted sloppy kisses on his face mask.

Hartman began to recognize individuals by size and shape or by the pattern of scars left on their backs by boat propellers. He gave them names, southern names, such as Pearly Mae and Flora Merry Lee, because they loved warm climates.

In 1979 Hartman's book about the manatee was published

Manatees feeding. The manatee is the only marine mammal that feeds exclusively on vegetation.   Patrick M. Rose

by the American Society of Mammalogists. It was called *Ecology and Behavior of the Manatee (Trichechus manatus) in Florida.*

Because of Dr. Hartman and the scientists who followed him, we know a great deal more about how the manatee spends its time.

For instance, we have learned that eating takes from six to eight hours a day, during which a large manatee will often consume over one hundred pounds of plants.

When it isn't eating, the manatee is often resting. For six to eight hours a day, for a few minutes or an hour at a time, it floats near the surface or lies on the bottom. Although its eyes are closed as if asleep, it is awake enough to rise at intervals to breathe.

Since it uses little energy while resting, the manatee needs less air than usual. It can stay underwater about ten to fifteen minutes, then goes gently to the surface and takes one to three breaths. After this it disappears without even a bubble to show where it has been. A manatee has the peculiar ability to sink into the water without expelling air or moving its tail or flippers, as if riding an elevator. This is possible because of unusually powerful muscles in its diaphragm which are able to compress the air it has inhaled.

While floating, its tail and flippers hang down. On the bottom, it supports itself by chin, stomach, and tail, turning over now and then the way people do when they sleep.

Manatees play off and on during the day and night. Young calves, three and four-year-olds, and adults often frolic together. They hug each other with their flippers, do somersaults and handstands, chase, bump, and kiss each other.

Biologists think kissing may be a way of greeting or a help in recognizing each other. Or perhaps they simply enjoy it.

Manatees are generally solitary, but at times they may form a group of a dozen or more. This is often true when a female, or cow, is in estrus, that is, when she is fertile and ready to mate. Then the adult males, or bulls, gather to court her. The cow swims away in a zigzag course, and the bulls follow. This may go on for one to four weeks. During this long competition, the bulls do not fight, although they often bump or push each other out of the way. At last the female stops fleeing and accepts the males one at a time.

The strongest, most lasting relationship in a manatee's life is with its mother. The cow, about to give birth after twelve to fourteen months of pregnancy, finds a private place. There the calf is born. Soon after, the sixty-to-seventy-pound infant swims to the surface for the first breath of air, with its mother following protectively.

The father does not seem to take part in the care of the baby. Males and females do not stay together as mates.

For up to two years the cow and calf stay close to each other, acting like friends and playmates. Often the calf rides on its mother's back. If both rest on the river bottom, the baby makes itself comfortable on her flat tail. During this two-year period

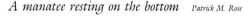

A manatee resting on the bottom   Patrick M. Rose

A young manatee with its mother Patrick M. Rose

the infant nurses from nipples beneath the mother's flippers, and gradually adds underwater grasses to its diet.

Whenever the calf swims away too far, the mother calls it back. Both cow and calf keep in constant touch with squeals and squeaks in an underwater duet. Although, like most marine animals, manatees have no outside ears, they seem to hear well. An infant has been known to respond to its mother's call when she is two hundred feet away.

In case of danger, the mother puts herself between her calf and the danger, or urges it to flee. But devoted as she is, she will not fight, even to protect her offspring.

Probably during this time of closeness, the calf, by following its mother, learns many things it needs to know, such as where to find food and what to eat. Eventually, the calf swims away, apparently ready to take care of itself.

One of the things the calf seems to learn is to travel with the seasons. In the United States the majority of the manatees winter in Florida. On rare occasions in the summer some move as far north as Virginia and the Carolinas, as far west as Louisiana.

A female manatee with nursing calf Patrick M. Rose

When a manatee decides on a winter resort it has almost as many choices as the human tourist. It can move farther south or, if it prefers, can swim up a river where warm springs temper the water. Like all tourists, weather is not its only reason for choosing a winter resort. The manatee also looks for a place that is quiet and where the meals are satisfactory.

The Crystal River on the central west coast of Florida is one of many popular manatee sanctuaries (refuges, safe places) that excel in both warmth and food. Here, and at Blue Spring Run and other manatee sanctuaries, there are important benefits. The speed of boats is controlled and in some areas motorboats are excluded.

According to James A. Powell, research specialist for the New York Zoological Society, the arrival of manatees in the Crystal River depends on the temperature of the Gulf of Mexico into which the river flows. In cold weather when Gulf waters are too cool for comfort, manatees travel about five miles upstream to the main spring in King's Bay, the source of the river. There they bask in the constant water temperature of 72 to 73 degrees F and feast on the plentiful supply of underwater grasses and plants.

Even in this almost ideal place, the wintering manatee may be disturbed by an overly friendly snorkeler or may have to dodge the motorboats that are allowed in most parts of the river. However, here, as well as in all sanctuaries where powerboats are allowed, the Department of Natural Resources, Florida Marine Patrol, and the U.S. Fish & Wildlife Service strictly monitor the speed.

In northeastern Florida, manatees flock to Blue Spring Run.

This sanctuary, a branch of the St. John's River, has a year-round temperature of 72 degrees F and is roped off to prevent entry of motorboats. Rangers give human visitors talks about the manatee and point out by name many that return each winter.

Not all winter havens for manatees are supplied by nature. Some are inadvertently provided by man. In recent years, power plants in various parts of Florida, discharging warm water into canals as part of the process of producing power, have attracted hordes of manatees. The warm canals give these animals, sensitive to cold, additional places to go in the winter or in case of a sudden freeze. Some people are not sure if this arrangement is all good. What if the power plant has an emergency and has to shut down?

Unaware of the pros and cons, every winter the manatees seek out such man-made sanctuaries and show up at power plants by the hundreds. In a *Life* magazine article, Patrick Rose, Marine Mammal Coordinator for the Department of Natural Resources, quipped, "Wouldn't you go to a power company if you were cold?"

The Florida Power & Light Company has proved to be a dependable friend to its underwater clients. Besides supplying funds for manatee research, in times of sudden cold its branch plants have sometimes turned on extra turbines to raise the temperature in the canals. The company also has decided on a policy of doing turbine maintenance in warm weather when a shutdown would not endanger the manatees.

Manatee,
Beware!

The manatees and their relatives have had a long, difficult history. For thousands of years they were hunted for their meat and hides. Today, although they are not as often killed for food, many die each year for various reasons. All Sirenia are in danger of disappearing from the earth.

Manatees are slow movers. Richard (Kipp) Frohlich, Marine Mammal Biologist with the Department of Natural Resources (DNR) describes them as "laid back." They often are injured or killed because they do not move fast enough to escape speeding boats.

In 1987 the DNR found 113 manatee bodies in Florida

waters. The number increased to 133 in 1988. Some of the deaths were natural, but a large proportion were directly or indirectly caused by man.

The manatee is most vulnerable when it rises to the surface to breathe. If a motorboat approaches slowly, the manatee usually hears it coming and moves out of the way or sinks to the bottom. However, in shallow water, if the boat is big, like a yacht or barge, going to the bottom may not be enough to save the creature. It may be crushed by the hull of the boat or cut by the propeller blades.

Frontal view of a manatee   Patrick M. Rose

Although the smaller high-speed boats are not as deadly as the larger craft, they, too, inflict many wounds and can also cause deaths. These fast boats do not give the manatee a chance. By the time the animal is aware the boat is coming, it is already too late.

The manatees swimming around with scars are the lucky ones. Their wounds have healed. Many less fortunate have died because the blades cut too deeply or the impact of the hull caused too much damage to the body.

The propeller-driven boat is not the manatee's only people-caused hazard. The shallow waters of the rivers and bays are dotted with small buoys which tell the boater to beware, a crab trap is below. A wire or one-fourth-inch polypropylene line fastens the buoy to the trap. Fishermen set out these traps, baited with chicken necks or other food attractive to crabs. Every day they pull up the trap, usually a square or oblong wire cage, to remove the crabs they have caught and to restock the bait.

Of course, the manatee doesn't know what the buoy means. Being curious, it swims around the trap, mouths it, nibbles at the algae which sometimes grow on the wire or line, then cruises on. Every now and then one catches a flipper on the line. Thrashing around, trying to get free, the captive succeeds only in wrapping the line more firmly around the base of the flipper. The manatee may swim for days, dragging the trap and buoy, while the line becomes tighter. This may eventually cause the loss of a flipper or even death from infection.

Among other dangers to the manatee are discarded fishing lines or lures that a manatee may swallow or that may hook into a tail or flipper and cause infection.

The scar on this manatee's flipper is the result of an injury caused by a crab trap line. Patrick M. Rose

A number of manatees have been injured or killed when caught in flood control gates or locks located in rivers or canals where they swim. Since the manatee has to surface at intervals to breathe, it is sometimes drowned when caught between the closing gates of a lock.

Biologist John E. Reynolds watched a mother and calf at a flood control dam. When he first saw them, they were above the dam. Two days later the pair were at the same dam, only this time the gates were open far enough for the calf to go through, but not wide enough for the mother to follow. For three hours the calf stayed in the water below the dam and the mother remained upstream, close to the partially open gates. All the time they waited, the two chirped and squealed to each other. As soon as the gates opened wider, the mother rushed to join her calf.

Some manatees, not as fortunate as the two above, are drowned when they try to go through gates that are not open wide enough or when a strong current holds them against the gates. Experiments are being carried out to try to prevent such accidents, and already improvements have been made.

Skin divers sometimes thoughtlessly chase manatees, not intending to harm them. But when the manatees swim away to

Manatee mothers are very protective of their young.   Patrick M. Rose

escape, a mother may be separated from her calf. At times, the frightened group of manatees ends up in waters where the food is not as plentiful or the water as warm as the place from which they were driven. Water colder than 68 degrees F is a danger to them. Their bodies cannot adjust to it, and it can lead to their deaths.

In the United States for many years it has been against the law to kill the manatee for food or for any other reason, but occasionally it still happens. On July 14, 1987, the body of a ten-and-one-half-foot-long manatee was found in Chokoloskee Bay in southwestern Florida. It had been shot through the head and cleaned of its meat. The maximum penalty for such a crime is a twenty-thousand-dollar fine and one year in prison.

When it comes to injuries or deaths other than natural, most are accidents. However, at times the manatee is tormented or deliberately injured. Being unafraid of humans, manatees often come to docks or close to shore where people can easily hurt or even kill them.

All of the above hazards are whittling away at the approximately 1,200 remaining West Indian manatees in Florida, but one final danger is the most deadly of all. The destruction of the manatees' habitat by waterfront development and pollution is leaving them fewer and fewer places to live.

With so many dangers, the manatee needs help.

Humans to the Rescue

People are often a threat to the manatee, but there are many who care. The way they devote their time, knowledge, and resources to helping it survive proves a human can be a manatee's best friend. The following are three accounts out of the many efforts that are made to help injured manatees.

On April 17, 1976, a young male manatee was picked up with a crab trap line around his left flipper and taken to Sea World of Florida for emergency treatment.

Henry, as he was named by rescuers, came from the Indian River near Titusville on the east coast of Florida. When he reached Sea World his flipper was so swollen and infected the veterinarian who was called in to examine him feared it would have to be amputated. At once the doctor treated the wound that encircled the flipper with antiseptics and administered antibiotics.

Animal specialists at Sea World of Florida remove crab trap line from Henry's flipper. Courtesy Sea World of Florida

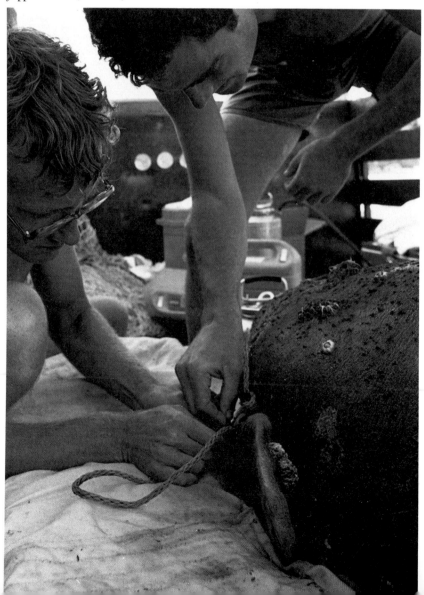

That first day Henry was in the pool at Sea World, although he was offered food, he did not eat. The place was new to him and no doubt he was in pain from his badly injured flipper.

The manatees' favorite food, underwater grasses, was not available at Sea World, so the staff improvised. The next day a tempting salad bar was spread out in the pool. Knowing that manatees usually prefer to eat plants from the bottoms of the rivers, Sea World staff members not only floated iceberg lettuce, endive, escarole, and romaine lettuce on top of the water, they also threaded the same type of food on a nylon rope on the floor of the pool where it was weighted and tied down.

Henry made it clear that he was hungry. In spite of his injured flipper, he dived to the bottom and began to eat. That day he devoured approximately five and one-half pounds of food. For his first week at Sea World he ate from the bottom of the pool. After that, he began feeding from the surface.

According to the report prepared by Edward D. Asper and Stan W. Searles of the Sea World staff, these were the foods offered to Henry in the order of his preference: (1) romaine lettuce (2) iceberg lettuce (3) endive (4) escarole, cabbage, spinach (5) carrot tops (6) water hyacinths. Henry ate water hyacinths only when they were the sole food in the pool, and then he just sampled the roots.

When Henry's wound was healed, he had good use of his flipper and was eating well, so the Sea World animal specialists decided to release him. During his stay of less than three months at Sea World, the manatee had gained fifty pounds.

In July he was painlessly freeze-marked on his back with a capital H to make it possible to keep track of him when he returned to the wild.

On July 9, 1976, Henry was released in the Indian River near the capture site. On many occasions after this, officers of the Florida Marine Patrol observed him swimming there.

A different type of manatee injury occurred in southwestern Florida. On February 4, 1979, several people in a mobile home park near the city of Fort Myers saw a manatee floating in one of the canals that reach out like long fingers from the Caloosahatchee River. These canals, filled with water from the nearby river, make it possible for boaters to travel from their own docks west to the Gulf of Mexico or east to the Atlantic Ocean.

The injured manatee, which seemed too weak to swim, rolled in the water near the bank of the canal.

One resident of the park remarked, "It almost turned belly up the way fish do when they're dying."

A call was made to the Florida Marine Patrol.

Watching the manatee with concern, residents of the park noticed dark forms in the water with it. Now and then a nose surfaced. Manatees!

Then, according to the reports of many of the people who lined the banks, a manatee swam to the one that was floundering. It dived under the injured animal, pushing it up so that its head rose above the water far enough for it to take a breath of air.

Witnesses stated that every now and then one of the other manatees repeated this process and sometimes, with the help of their flippers, seemed to try to keep their weakened comrade right side up.

When Lieutenant (now Major) Denis Grealish of the Florida Marine Patrol observed what was happening, he stayed, waiting for assistance. "Right then," Major Grealish later said, "I couldn't have done any more than the other manatees were doing for him."

In the meantime, the Florida Marine Patrol had contacted Sea World and Dr. Gary Nelson, a Fort Myers veterinarian with experience in caring for dolphins and sea lions and a frequent volunteer in cases of need. Dr. Nelson arrived at the park with two other men who also understood how to deal with marine animals.

Dr. Nelson examined the ill manatee and reported it had been hit in the side by a boat, injuring the chest and lung. He expressed horror at the animal's weight loss. He said it was half as big around as it should have been for its length.

The other manatees had drawn back when the doctor and his two associates entered the water. They made no effort to interfere, but they did not leave, even when Dr. Nelson took over the task of keeping the injured manatee breathing. Timing the intervals with his watch, he lifted its head so it could get the breaths of air it needed.

By the time a truck from Sea World arrived from Orlando, Dr. Nelson had been in the chilly water three hours. The manatee was still breathing, though not showing any improvement in its condition.

The two animal care specialists from Sea World brought with them a nylon stretcher. Assisted by eight other men, several of them from the mobile home park, they slid it under the injured manatee and pulled it onto the bank of the canal. Then the ten men, all lifting together, raised the manatee onto a thick mat in the truck. There it was wrapped with moist coverings. At once

A manatee is transported on a stretcher in a sling. Patrick M. Rose

the two animal specialists from Sea World began their examination and testing.

When the truck pulled away, the waiting manatees slowly left. So did the people who lined the shores of the canal.

At Sea World, the manatee was given medication to try to cure the pneumonia it had contracted as a result of the injuries. However, its lung was too badly damaged, and a few days later it died. Manatees and humans had done all they could, but it was not enough.

On October 29, 1987, answering a call from a concerned fisherman, Kipp Frohlich, Marine Mammal Biologist, hurried to the point where the power company's warm water discharge canal runs into the Orange River near the city of Fort Myers. There he found a manatee with a crab trap fastened firmly in front of his body with the line around both flippers.

Frohlich swam toward the creature, hoping to untangle the lines, but the manatee swam away. The biologist then called Sea World's beached animal recovery team.

The next day the team arrived, placed a net across the power

Biologists are capturing an injured manatee. This one is strong enough to put up a fight. Patrick M. Rose

canal, and chased the manatee into it. They then put a stretcher under him and carried him to a truck where the lines and trap were removed. Soon he was on his way to the Manatee Rehabilitation Facility at Sea World of Florida near Orlando.

According to a report in the *Island Observer*, a newspaper published on Sanibel Island, Florida, Dan Odell, Staff Research Biologist at Sea World, said, "The rope was wrapped so tightlly that the flippers were swollen. But he responded well to treatment, and there weren't any broken bones in the flippers. He was lucky."

The manatee, named Myers because he was found near Fort Myers, stayed sixteen months at Sea World. According to Frohlich, the manatee weighed 625 pounds when he was picked up and 826 pounds at the end of his stay.

On March 8, 1989, Myers, now healthy and with flippers healed, was released in the same power canal where he had been picked up. Hoping to keep track of him and make sure he was able to adjust to life in the wild, the biologists fastened on his tail a radio transmitter developed by the U.S. Fish & Wildlife Service.

With the help of this transmitter, Kipp Frohlich was able to follow Myers from the Orange River to the mouth of the Caloosahatchee River where it enters San Carlos Bay.

"He was eating sea grasses and was in the company of another manatee," said Frohlich.

Two days later Myers was seen forty miles north in the Peace River, still wearing the transmitter. It was clear that he was strong and able to care for himself. One more manatee had been saved.

How
Science Can Help

The small plane, a Cesna 172, flew low over a river in southern Florida. The two men in the cockpit were taking photos and counting manatees.

From the air a manatee usually shows up clearly. Marine Mammal Biologist Kipp Frohlich once said, "It looks something like an Idaho potato with flippers."

The plane angled still lower.

"Look at those scars," said one of the men. "Recognize them?"

His companion peered through binoculars at the pattern of propeller marks on the back of the manatee. "I sure do. That's

Aerial views help biologists count manatees and locate injured or dead ones.

Patrick M. Rose

Winston, number eighty-five." He made a note on his pad. "Last time I saw him he was in the Gulf. Winston gets around."

The two men are biologists with the Florida Department of Natural Resources (DNR) which works closely with the U.S. Fish & Wildlife Service (USF&WS), sharing the task of state-wide surveying.

While counting manatees and finding out where they live, the scientists identify as many as possible by some mark or unusual feature of the body, then assign a number. Some of the best known also have names. Since a large percentage bear propeller scars, that is a common way of telling them apart.

The biologists also watch for manatees that are injured, in trouble, or dead. In the case of the ones which need help, they arrange for aid to be sent. When a dead manatee is located, a postmortem is performed by a specialist connected with the DNR or the USF&WS. By examining the bodies, the cause of death can usually be determined. This information could lead to better manatee protection.

The air survey may include tracking manatees by radio telemetry. Often before releasing one which has recovered from injury or illness, a color-coded antenna with a small transmitter

This manatee is wearing a radio transmitter on its tail. Patrick M. Rose

attached is fastened to its tail, so it can be followed and observed. In some cases a satellite transmitter shaped like a coffee can with colored bars is used.

For the safety of the animal, the transmitter is fastened to the tail with a weak link that will break if snagged, and is corrodible so that the harness will eventually drop off. The range of the radio transmitter is five miles in water, thirty-five miles in the air. Since radio waves do not travel far in water, the biologist fastens the antenna to the harness on a tether that allows it to float. In six feet of water or less, it will be above the surface.

This mother manatee has a radio transmitter on her tail. Her calf swims by her side. Patrick M. Rose

If you see either kind of antenna mysteriously moving along just above the water, look carefully at the color stripes so you can describe them. Then phone the toll-free Manatee Hotline of the DNR, 1-800-342-1821, and report what you have seen. The line is manned by the DNR's Florida Marine Patrol (FMP), the organization that, in addition to law enforcement on land and water, handles calls concerning marine animals. Your information can help them locate a tagged manatee.

This hotline number can also be used by anyone who sees a dead or injured manatee or one that needs help for any reason. When such a call comes in, at once a representative of the FMP investigates the problem and, if help is needed, a call is made to Sea World at Orlando, the Miami Seaquarium, or other appropriate agency.

In Florida the head of DNR's wide-ranging program for marine mammals is Marine Mammal Coordinator Patrick Rose, who has a master's degree in aquatic biology. He has worked vigorously for the manatee for many years and also understands human needs. In an interview for the August, 1987, issue of *Save the Manatee Club News*, Rose said he hoped to "contribute to successful protection of the aquatic resources that manatees depend on, as well as other aquatic species, while realistically accommodating controlled growth within the state of Florida."

Besides its field work and many other activities to help the manatee, the DNR, along with the Florida Audubon Society, sponsors the Save the Manatee Club.

On November 14, 1984, the club's Adopt-a-Manatee program was opened by then Florida Governor Robert Graham and Save the Manatee Committee Chairman, singer and songwriter Jimmy Buffett. At a modest cost an individual or a classroom can adopt a manatee, choosing from a list of those that winter at Blue Spring State Park in eastern Florida. The adopter will receive a photograph of his own manatee and information on its life history. Money earned by this program is used to help protect and preserve manatees and pay for research on them.

To learn more about the Save the Manatee Club or the Adopt-a-Manatee program see "For More About the Manatee" in the back of this book.

Dr. Thomas J. O'Shea is Sirenia Project Leader of the National Ecology Research Center of the U.S. Fish & Wildlife Service. The group he heads does important research work on the manatee. The Sirenia Project studies manatee migrations and habitat needs, manatee behavioral communication, and their basic population biology. They work on radio telemetry and do aerial surveys of manatees. They also cooperate in manatee research and conservation training with people in other countries.

Sign posted by
Save the Manatee Club

Patrick M. Rose

The USF&WS did pioneer research on the manatee and continues to add to our knowledge of this threatened mammal.

Through the years laws have been passed for the good of the endangered manatee. The United States Marine Mammal Protection Act which became law in December, 1972, prevents the taking of manatees within United States waters. They may be captured for display or research purposes only with a permit from the Secretary of the Interior.

The Endangered Species Act of 1973 did even more to help, demanding that both state and federal governments work out a plan for protecting the manatees' habitat and increasing their numbers.

In 1978 the Florida State Legislature passed the Florida Manatee Sanctuary Act, making the whole state a manatee sanctuary.

Dr. Jesse White is another person who is dedicated to helping the manatee. For a long time Dr. White, then veterinarian at the Miami Seaquarium, had dreamed of breeding and raising manatees in captivity and eventually releasing them to a free life. This, he reasoned, would help to change the dark future of the species. The problem was that the Seaquarium's two adult manatees, Romeo and Juliet, mated but did not produce any offspring.

Then Dr. White had an idea. Diet affected reproduction of land animals that lived on grasses and plants. They often needed additional nutrients. Perhaps this was true of marine animals, too.

He began to feed his manatees extra calcium and phosphorous, and added apples, bananas, and carrots to the lettuce and cabbage they usually ate. Romeo and Juliet seemed to enjoy their new menu and in a short time Juliet became pregnant. About fourteen months later she gave birth to Lorelei, the first manatee to be conceived and born in captivity.

This was an encouraging forward step, but Dr. White and other scientists soon realized that captive breeding was not the answer to saving the manatee from extinction. For one thing it was too slow. It would take a large number of captive manatees, all busily producing offspring at the usual rate of one every two or three years, to offset even a fraction of those that died annually.

Besides, the new calves must be fed and cared for until they were old enough to be set free. This would be costly.

And how could the young, bred and raised in captivity, learn to live in the strange, competitive world of rivers and coastal waters? Sick or injured animals, picked up from the rivers and streams and nursed back to health, were habitually released in the same area where they were found. The captive-born had no home in the wild to which they could return.

In spite of all the problems and questions, the captive breeding program continued.

On August 8, 1984, Sunrise, a male manatee, and Savannah, a female, both born and raised at the Miami Seaquarium and both almost two years old, were moved to Homosassa Springs Nature World in western Florida. Their new home was a large, sectioned-off part of the Homosassa River where they could become accustomed to a natural way of life. Their diet was hydrilla and other aquatic plants. The two manatees quickly began eating the natural food and had no trouble adjusting to life in the river. With the help and cooperation of J.P. Garner,

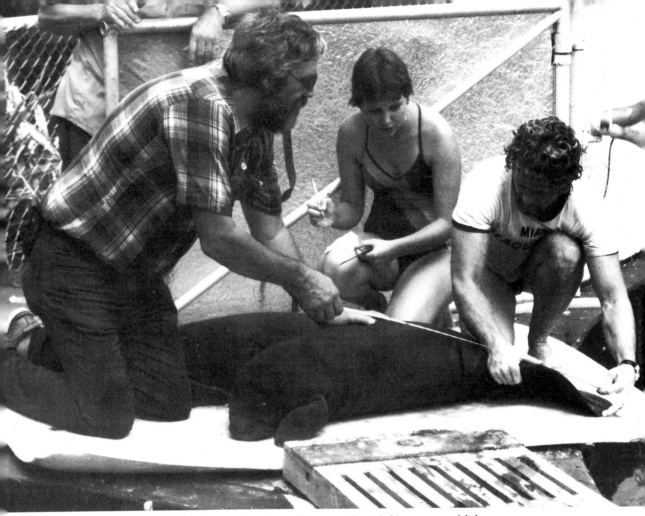

Dr. Jesse White measures Sunrise and Savannah with his rescue and lab assistants looking on   Courtesy Miami Seaquarium

manager of Homosassa Springs Nature World, the manatees had a "halfway house," as Dr. White called it.

On March 28, 1986, the gate in the river was opened for Sunrise and Savannah, the first manatees born in captivity to be released into the wild. They swam away together, wearing radio tracking devices on their tails. Both were tracked by radio until mid-April, then all contact was lost.

Savannah's tether and radio tag were found July 25, 1986, by a Fish & Wildlife Service biologist. The tether had broken loose at the weak link that is built into it so if it catches on some object the manatee will be able to swim free. Savannah has never been resighted and is assumed by many to be dead.

On November 11, 1986, Sunrise's transmitter and tether were found intact by men on a shrimp trawler five to six miles offshore in the Gulf of Mexico. Investigators believe the manatee might have gone too far out, became disoriented, and possibly starved.

Manatee specialists involved in the program decided that captive-born manatees, never having lived in the wild, may be unable to adjust to the natural world. They agreed these manatees should not be released or, at any rate, not until more research has been done.

Such manatees, along with others that are recovering from injuries or illness, are now kept at Homosassa Springs, Sea World, the Miami Seaquarium, or in other protected facilities where they can be studied at all stages of their lives.

Juliet, still living at the Miami Seaquarium, gave birth to her sixth calf on March 13, 1989, setting a record for the most recorded births for one manatee mother.

Although manatees do not perform tricks as sea lions and dolphins do, people enjoy watching these friendly mammals as they go through their daily lives swimming, diving, eating, sleeping, and playing together. Unknowingly, they are the actors in a living theater where people can come to learn about them and their needs.

Is There
Hope?

At present there is an uneasy balance between estimated manatee births and known deaths, holding the population in Florida waters to approximately 1,200, or perhaps a few more.

Can that figure, a small fraction of the number that once lived in the area, be maintained, or possibly increased? Or will some change in the habits of man or nature reduce the manatee count to zero?

Some signs are favorable for survival. More and more people are interested, as evidenced by programs on public television, articles in newspapers, and in national magazines such as *National Geographic* and *Reader's Digest*.

Manatee sculpture on the Caloosahatchee River gets a cleaning by firemen from Fort Myers. Garth Francis/News Press

Personnel at Sea World, Homosassa Springs Nature World, and the Miami Seaquarium actively care for the manatee in health and illness and constantly work for its welfare.

In schools children write essays on the manatee and classrooms adopt a manatee through the Save the Manatee Club.

Even in the field of the arts there is evidence of interest. Manatee posters are on sale in stores. An airy aluminum sculpture of two manatees stands in the Caloosahatchee River at Fort Myers, Florida. Dedicated by artist Rick Baquero (Tiite) "with love and pride to the life and work of Dr. Jesse White," it is a lasting reminder to boaters that living creatures just beneath the surface need their consideration.

Captive births are important not, as was hoped, as a means of building up manatee population, but because they are useful for research on manatees and provide a way of helping people of all ages to learn about them and their needs.

United States and Florida governments are trying to save the natural, undeveloped lands and prevent pollution of lakes, rivers, and streams. This helps to preserve the manatees' habitat.

Speed caution sign near a power plant   Patrick M. Rose

Many organizations and individuals work to protect the manatee and make people aware that it is in danger of disappearing.

The manatee has strong legal protection. Signs are put up each year in marinas and along rivers where manatees gather, announcing that boaters must slow down. The speed limit varies according to the location or time of year. DNR's Florida Marine Patrol enforces these speed regulations.

Although much is being done for the manatee, if we continue to build on and pollute waterways where they live, travel fast on their rivers, and destroy the wild lands, they are doomed.

But they do not have to vanish. If many people had fought to save Steller's sea cow or the passenger pigeon, they might still be here. Today, if enough people care enough, there can be manatees for the men, women, and children of the twenty-first century to enjoy.

For More About the Manatee

Florida Department of Natural
   Resources (DNR)
Office of Communications
Marjory Stoneman Douglas
   Building
3900 Commonwealth Boulevard
Tallahasse, Florida 32302

United States Fish & Wildlife
   Service (USF&WS)
Jacksonville Field Office
3100 University Boulevard
   South
Suite 120
Jacksonville, Florida 32216

Florida Game & Freshwater
   Fish Commission
   (FG&FWFC)
Endangered Species Coordinator
Farris Bryant Building
620 S. Meridian Street
Tallahassee, Florida 32301

Florida Audubon Society (FAS)
1101 Audubon Way
Maitland, Florida 32751

Save the Manatee Club (SMC)
500 N. Maitland Avenue
Maitland, Florida 32751

Florida Power & Light
  Company (FP&L)
Corporate Communications
P.O. Box 529100
Miami, Florida 33152

Miami Seaquarium
4400 Rickenbacker Causeway
Miami, Florida 33149

Sea World of Florida
Education Department
7007 Sea World Drive
Orlando, Florida 32809

Florida Department of
  Environmental Regulation
  (DER)
Office of Public Information
2600 Blairstone Road
Tallahassee, Florida 32301

Homosassa Springs State Park
P.O. Box 189
Homosassa Springs, Florida
  32647

United States Department of the
  Interior
Fish & Wildlife Service
Chassahowitzka National
  Wildlife Refuge
Route 2, Box 44
Homosassa, Florida 32646
*Ask for information on manatee
  refuges.*

Florida Department of Natural
  Resources
Florida Marine Research
  Institute
100 Eighth Avenue S.E.
St. Petersburg, Florida 33701

Index